The National Archives

The Buildings That Made London

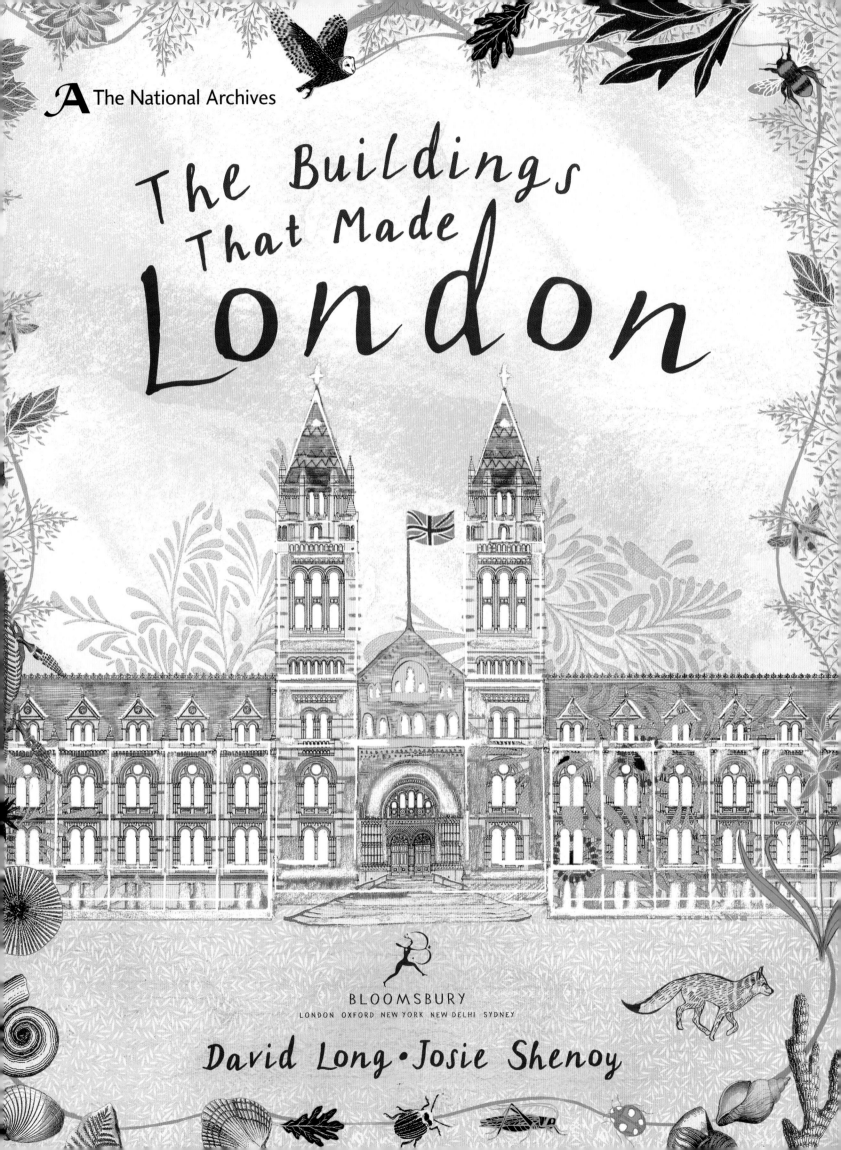

BLOOMSBURY
LONDON OXFORD NEW YORK NEW DELHI SYDNEY

David Long • Josie Shenoy

Contents

Introduction

Originally a Roman trading post on the north bank of the Thames, London's history is a long one and its architectural heritage is among the richest and most varied anywhere in the world.

Like any great city, London has never stopped evolving, and the familiar skyline seems to change almost every year. Each century has left its mark in brick and stone or steel and glass, and the demands of a growing population and a changing world mean London's architects and builders are always busy.

Despite wars and great fires many of the most famous buildings have survived hundreds of years. Others have been rebuilt or remodelled, sometimes more than once, and often exhibit more than one style of architecture. Some look the same as they always have;

some are barely recognisable. Using original architectural plans and drawings of these buildings from The National Archives, brought to life by vibrant artwork, this book allows us to cast our eyes back to the very beginning and shines a new light on a city we all think we know. As you watch each building transform and grow, you'll learn about its former inhabitants and the different roles it has played throughout history. This is the best way to appreciate the genius of those who created London, and to understand how it became the magnificent place it is today.

So, turn the page, step back in time and be amazed by what you discover.

Big Ben

The Palace of Westminster has three huge towers. The tallest of these is the great square Victoria Tower, standing 98.5 metres high. The most famous is the Elizabeth Tower, often known as 'Big Ben', which is really the name of the largest of the tower's five bells.

Big Ben is around two metres shorter than the Victoria Tower but looks slightly taller because it is slimmer. The tower is home to the Great Clock of Westminster which, with its four faces, is the most famous clock in the world. Everything about Big Ben is huge! The mechanism alone weighs five tons and when the 13.7-ton main bell was first installed it took 18 hours to winch it 60 metres up the tower.

The clock was designed by Edmund Beckett Dennison, a Victorian lawyer whose hobby was horology (the study of watches and other timepieces). Despite being an amateur, in 1851 he came up with the design for an incredibly precise mechanism.

When the clock was completed eight years later it was found to be accurate to within one second a day. Londoners still set their watches by listening out for the chimes of Big Ben!

In July 2012 Big Ben chimed more than 30 times. This was to welcome the world's athletes to the capital for the 30th Olympic Games.

In 1949, the clock was found to be running several minutes slow. This was because a flock of starlings had been perching on one of the minute hands!

The chimes are broadcast live on BBC Radio 4 every evening at six o'clock. Bizarrely, because sound travels relatively slowly, anyone standing at the foot of the tower listening to the radio hears the chimes being broadcast before they hear the real thing!

During the First and Second World Wars the clock faces were not lit up at night. It was feared that the lights might be used to guide enemy bombers to central London.

Admiralty Arch

Admiralty Arch is the ceremonial entrance to the Mall (leading up to Buckingham Palace) from Trafalgar Square. It forms a barrier between the noisy chaos of Trafalgar Square and the quiet formality around Buckingham Palace. The graceful curve of the Arch forms part of Sir Aston Webb's great scheme to remodel Buckingham Palace into the world famous landmark we all recognize today.

It was built at a time when the British Empire was at its most powerful, encompassing a quarter of the world and its people. Webb designed the Mall as the starting point for a magnificent royal processional route through London, from Buckingham Palace to St Paul's Cathedral.

Traffic flows through the left- and right-hand arches. However, the central arch is kept locked and is only used on important ceremonial occasions.

Today, above the three main gateways, a luxury hotel enables guests to enjoy spectacular views of the colour and pageantry associated with royal weddings and other great state occasions. However, as the name suggests, the building was originally part of the Admiralty.

The head of the Royal Navy, the splendidly-named First Sea Lord, traditionally has his London home here. Over the years the Admiralty Arch has had lots of important residents, including former British Prime Minister Winston Churchill and Admiral Sir Terence Lewin.

The Latin inscription on the arch reads, 'In the tenth year of the reign of King Edward VII, to Queen Victoria from a grateful nation'.

A stone carving of a nose is fixed to one of the pillars. The story goes that this is Napoleon's or the Duke of Wellington's nose, and troops touch it for good luck. In fact it was put there only a few years ago by a cheeky artist!

Banqueting House

In 1512 King Henry VIII moved from the Palace of Westminster into the Palace of Whitehall. With 1,500 rooms it was the largest palace in Europe at the time and was often compared to a small town! Henry died here in 1547 and his successors continued to expand and improve the palace. However in 1688 when William III and Mary II were on the throne, the Royal Family abandoned Whitehall in favour of the smaller, prettier Kensington Palace. Within ten years Whitehall had suffered several catastrophic fires. Today the Banqueting House is the largest surviving fragment. Built for James I by Inigo Jones in 1622, it is the most modern part of

This building replaced an earlier Banqueting House, which had been accidentally destroyed by a fire. Workmen clearing up after a New Year's party bizarrely decided to burn the rubbish inside the building!

Inigo Jones

the old palace and one of the most influential buildings in London's fascinating architectural history.

Jones made several trips to Italy during his lifetime to discover new ideas about architecture. He was probably the first Englishman ever to visit and sketch the ruins of ancient Rome. Jones was a follower of the Italian architect,

Andrea Palladio. Palladio introduced an entirely new style of architecture, called Neoclassicism. Jones brought the style to England. Inspired by the buildings of ancient Rome and Greece, the clean, elegant design of the Banqueting House was hugely popular and the style quickly spread through the country, replacing the old, gloomy Gothic and Tudor styles.

The building is perhaps most famous as the scene of Charles I's execution. In 1649 he stepped through one of the large first floor windows and was beheaded on a scaffold outside.

James I

11

British Museum

After the British Museum was founded in the 18th century it took over the Duke of Montagu's old house in Bloomsbury. The first visitors were admitted in 1759 and, to begin with, it was open for just three hours a day. Visitors had to write asking for an appointment, and only ten people were allowed in at a time! The displays at the museum included the Royal Library, which contained more than 10,000 books owned by various sovereigns from Henry VIII to Charles II. There were also works of art, thousands of plant and animal specimens, and historic manuscripts. All were donated by rich collectors or bought by the government. Now there is only room to show just one per cent of the museum's eight million objects. Many of the most precious objects

By 1900 the museum had its own station on the London Underground. When this closed in the 1930s the building and the tunnels beneath it were taken over by the army.

In 1879 the British Museum became the first public building in London to be lit by electricity.

can never be displayed because ordinary daylight would damage them.

By 1823 it was clear that the old house was too small and so several new galleries were designed by Sir Robert Smirke. The new buildings were designed in a style known as Greek Revival. Visitors now entered through a vast portico, styled like a Greek temple. Behind this Smirke created a large courtyard surrounding a circular, domed Reading Room. Designed by his brother Sydney, the Reading Room contained more than 25 miles of cast iron shelves. However, with the collections growing each year, the books were eventually moved to the new British Library.

Legend has it that the museum has a ghost. A mummy known only as 'an unnamed singer of Amen-Re' is said to have put a curse on its keepers. Its first owner vanished suddenly, the second was wounded in a shooting accident, and the third sold it on to the museum.

One of the most famous exhibits is the 2,200 year-old Rosetta Stone, discovered by a French soldier in Egypt. Confiscated after the defeat of the Emperor Napoleon, it was crucial in helping to decode Egyptian hieroglyphs.

10 Downing Street

Behind the world-famous black front door, the house known as No. 10 Downing Street has been home to Britain's Prime Ministers since 1735. These have included William Pitt the Younger, Sir Winston Churchill, Margaret Thatcher and Tony Blair. Most of the rooms are actually used as offices or to entertain important visitors. Because of this, the Prime Minister's family actually lives in quite a small flat near the top. A few Prime Ministers have preferred their own houses to No. 10, and in the 1960s Harold Wilson used to sneak home through a back door when the television cameras had gone.

For security reasons, No. 10 Downing Street is usually closed to members of the public. Journalists and television cameras are allowed in when the Prime Minister makes an important announcement, but most of the time the street is closed off from the public by a large set of black gates that are guarded by armed police.

From inside the house it is possible to enter the two neighbouring houses and all three share a private garden at the back. No. 11 is the official residence of another important government minister, the Chancellor of the Exchequer. It contains another flat for their family and there is a private corridor linking No. 10 to more offices inside No. 12.

DOWNING STREET SW1
CITY OF WESTMINSTER

Sir Robert Walpole

William Pitt the Younger

William Gladstone

Winston Churchill

Margaret Thatcher

Tony Blair

No. 10 was originally a gift from George II to the country's first Prime Minister, Sir Robert Walpole. He refused it and suggested that instead the house should be used by all future Prime Ministers.

Archaeologists have found evidence nearby of Roman, Anglo-Saxon and Norman settlements, showing that this area was already an important centre of government around 1,000 years ago.

During the Second World War No. 10 was damaged by several enemy bombs falling nearby. In 1991 terrorists fired a mortar bomb into the garden—this left a large crater but fortunately no one was hurt or injured.

Hampton Court Palace

This spectacular royal palace began as a simple medieval manor before it was rebuilt as England's grandest country house. It belonged to Cardinal Thomas Wolsey, Henry VIII's chief adviser, but was seized by the king after the two men quarrelled in 1529. Henry already had more than 60 houses but he was an enthusiastic builder and made Wolsey's palace even larger.

After Henry's death the palace continued to grow. In the late 17th century King William III asked Sir Christopher Wren to build him something to rival King Louis XIV of France's vast palace at Versailles. Wren threw himself into the project. He destroyed much of the Tudor palace, which by this time was considered to be deeply unfashionable. However, several courtyards

Charles I was a frequent visitor to the palace, but after his defeat in the Civil War he was imprisoned there in 1647. He managed to escape, but was recaptured and executed two years later.

Charles I

from the original building have survived, along with Henry's magnificent Great Hall.

Following the death of William III's wife Queen Mary II, in 1694, work stopped for a while. The palace was still an uninhabitable, empty brick shell and it was several years before work restarted. By the time William III died in 1702, Hampton Court Palace looked much as it does today.

Hampton Court Palace is sometimes described as a palace of two halves – one of them Tudor and the other elegantly Baroque. It is a history of English architecture in a single building.

William Shakespeare

James I enjoyed hunting in the park that surrounded the palace and used it as a venue for plays, parties and banquets. Performers included William Shakespeare, whose plays were sometimes performed in front of a royal audience.

James I

Cardinal Thomas Wolsey

THE ROYAL TENNIS COURT

Henry VIII was a keen tennis player. People still play an old-fashioned version of the game on the indoor court at Hampton Court Palace.

King Henry VIII

17

Horse Guards

Overlooking the Army's ceremonial parade ground, the 18th century building known as Horse Guards was designed by William Kent, an important architect who built some of England's finest country houses and landscaped gardens. Kent chose an Italian style of architecture called Palladian. When viewed from the bridge across the lake in nearby St James's Park (with the London Eye in the background) it lies at the centre of one of the most picturesque views in the capital.

For more than a century it has been the headquarters of the Household Cavalry, the name given to the two senior regiments of the British Army, which are responsible for protecting the Royal Family. The Household Cavalry are present at important ceremonial events in London

The Horse Guards building replaced an area called the tiltyard where Henry VIII frequently enjoyed watching and taking part in jousting tournaments.

and at Windsor Castle and play an active role in fighting overseas when the country is at war.

The central archway is the symbolic entrance to St James's Palace. For this reason, although members of the public may walk through it, the only people allowed to drive through are the reigning monarch and those issued with a rare, special pass from the Palace.

The public can visit parts of the building, which contains a museum on the long history of the regiments of the British Army and stables for the mounted guards' horses.

The two o'clock position on the clock above the archway is painted in black. It marks the precise time at which King Charles I was executed across the street at the Banqueting House on 30 January 1649.

Each day, between 10am and 4pm, two soldiers guard the central archway dressed in gleaming armour and seated on immaculately groomed horses. They change once an hour, or every 30 minutes in exceptionally cold weather.

Houses of Parliament

The Houses of Parliament were rebuilt following a disastrous fire in 1834. The fire destroyed the vast, sprawling Palace of Westminster, which dated back to the 11th century and the reign of King Edward the Confessor. Westminster Hall is one of the early parts of the palace that survived the fire.

The architect of the new building was Sir Charles Barry.

His design was chosen from nearly 100 rival schemes. His style, known as Neo-Gothic, gives the building its medieval appearance, which was a highly advanced design for the time.

Sir Charles Barry took charge of the mammoth project, but he left the lavish decoration of the building to fellow architect, Augustus Pugin, who designed every

The chamber of the House of Commons is surprisingly small, and can seat only 427 of the 650 MPs.

Augustus Pugin

Sir Charles Barry

Today guide dogs are the only animals allowed in the building — although it is widely known to be overrun with thousands of mice!

last detail himself, down to the locks on the doors, the wallpaper, and even the inkwells.

This took nearly 25 years and the effort destroyed both men. Pugin suffered a mental breakdown and died in a hospital for the care of the insane. After instructing his son to supervise the building's final stages, Sir Charles died just as the tallest of the building's three towers was nearing completion.

Today it is best known for its two debating chambers, the House of Commons (where Members of Parliament sit) and the House of Lords. These occupy only a small portion of the building, which has more than 1,100 other rooms, a hundred staircases and three miles of corridors!

The two nearest bridges, Westminster and Lambeth, are painted to match the green and red leather benches in the chambers of the Commons and the Lords.

Because MPs are traditionally barred from bringing a weapon into the chamber the lifts in the building still have special hooks to hang swords on.

Imperial War Museum

The Imperial War Museum was officially opened in 1920. At that time its task was to record the heroism and sacrifice of the people of Britain and its Empire during World War I.

The early years of the museum were spent in South-east London at Sydenham Hill, but in the 1930s it moved closer to the centre of the city. It now occupies what was once the Bethlem Royal Hospital.

The building itself is Georgian and was built in 1815 by James Lewis in the Neoclassical style. From the 1830s onwards it was modified and extended by Sydney Smirke, the architect of the British Museum.

The museum became an enemy target during the Second World War. In January 1941 a bomb destroyed one of several aeroplanes on display.

HEN · VIII · REGE · FVNDATV

Smirke built a large dome (with a chapel beneath) and long wings to provide increased accommodation for patients. The space beneath the dome now houses a reading room, which is often used by famous authors and film-makers who are looking for information to help with new projects.

Despite its age, the interior is strikingly modern. The large central hall or atrium displays jeeps, tanks, historic aircraft and even a rocket. The role of the museum has also evolved; it now honours British and Commonwealth troops in all wars.

Exhibits on display today include the world's largest collection of Victoria Cross medals – the highest military award for bravery.

VM·LARGITAS·PERFECIT.

The museum also includes the warship HMS Belfast, which is moored nearby on the River Thames.

Jewel Tower

Built around 1365, The Jewel Tower was surrounded by a moat to protect the precious contents inside. These included the royal jewels, ceremonial clothes belonging to King Edward III, valuable furs and gold and silver vessels.

The small three-storey tower is believed to be the work of Henry de Yevele. He was the successful master mason who built parts of Westminster Abbey and the Tower of London, as well as a number of important royal tombs. Kentish ragstone was used to build the tower, the same limestone the Romans had chosen more than a thousand years earlier to build a tall, defensive wall around the City of London.

From the outside it looks like a miniature fortress but the interior includes elaborate carved stone heads, birds and flowers. However, by 1600 the Jewel Tower had been transferred to the Clerk of the Parliaments and was used to store important documents from the House of Lords. Today it is a small museum containing objects from its long history, including an Iron Age sword.

King Edward III

Within the tower there are just two rooms on each storey with spiral staircases linking the different levels.

The material used to build the tower was brought up the Thames by barge. It took 98 boats to carry the stone from Kent with timber arriving from Surrey and red floor-tiles from Flanders (in what is now Belgium).

The contents of the tower belonged to the sovereign. Occasionally items might be removed to be presented as gifts to visiting monarchs, or used to raise funds if the king went off to fight a war.

In order to protect the contents there were no windows on the ground floor. An official keeper lived on the first floor and the treasures were stored safely on the floor above.

Palm House

One of London's most exotic buildings can be found in the Royal Botanic Gardens at Kew. The Palm House was built in the 18th century so horticulturalists could better our knowledge of how plants grow.

Kew is home to more than 30,000 different species of plants, collected from around the world, and about seven million preserved specimens are used for scientific study. Some of the largest and most impressive examples live here in the Victorian Palm House.

Architect Richard Turner learned many of his techniques working in shipbuilding. This is why the Palm House looks a bit like the upturned hull of an old-fashioned boat.

Richard Turner

This vast structure is the work of architects Decimus Burton and Richard Turner. Turner was a specialist in building using wrought iron. In the 1840s Burton and Turner created a lofty frame of metal arches. These were held together by a complex network of cables and tubes and held about 16,000 individual panes of glass.

As the name suggests, the building is home to Kew's tropical palm trees, which reach the top of the 18-metre-high building. High walkways make it possible for visitors to look down on the trees, almost as if you are flying above a vibrant rainforest.

The statues of ten mythical creatures outside the Palm House are copies of the 'Queen's Beasts'. The originals stood outside Westminster Abbey for Her Majesty's Coronation in 1953.

Decimus Burton

National Gallery

As Britain's largest and most visited art gallery, the National Gallery has around 1,000 paintings on display at any one time, the oldest of which date back more than 700 years.

The idea for The National Gallery first came about in the 1820s when the government bought 38 pictures from a collector called John Julius Angerstein. These were displayed at his house in Pall Mall until a new building was built overlooking Trafalgar Square.

The architect of the new gallery was William Wilkins, who also designed University College London in Bloomsbury. King William IV didn't like the finished building at all, and called it a 'nasty little pokey hole'. It was quickly modified and then expanded several times as more and more paintings were added to the national collection.

These extensions meant that many famous architects worked on the National Gallery at different times. These include James Pennethorne, who also designed the ballroom

John Julius Angerstein

During the Second World War many of the most valuable paintings were removed from the gallery to keep them safe from enemy air raids. They were secretly stored in a disused Welsh slate mine.

THE NA

THE NATIONAL GALLERY

Michelangelo

Claude Monet

at Buckingham Palace, and Edward Barry, whose father Charles was the architect of the Houses of Parliament. The newest extension was designed by an American architect called Robert Venturi.

Today, as a result of this gradual expansion, the National Gallery fills one whole side of the Trafalgar Square and it takes several hours to explore! However, it is still much too small to display all of the pictures it owns and so around 1,500 of them are kept in storage.

Robert Venturi

James Pennethorne

Edward Barry

Most of the paintings are by famous artists from other countries. Since 1897 works by British artists have been displayed at Tate Britain.

In 1914 the Rokeby Venus, a magnificent painting by the Spanish artist Diego Velázquez, was damaged by a visitor protesting at the refusal of the government to give women the right to vote.

Diego Velázquez

VOTES FOR WOMEN

Vincent Van Gogh

Leonardo da Vinci

Natural History Museum

The Natural History Museum was originally part of the British Museum but was moved to its own home in South Kensington in 1881. The architect of the new building was Alfred Waterhouse, who designed many important Victorian buildings (including St Pancras Station and the 19th century's largest country house).

For the new museum, Waterhouse chose a style called Romanesque Revival. This used the most up-to-date materials and methods but took its inspiration from buildings of the 11th and 12th centuries. The most striking thing about the exterior of the museum, besides its immense size, is the use of colourful tiles of glazed terracotta or

The museum already had so many exhibits that even two years after the building opened, staff were still busy moving boxes across from the British Museum.

Buckingham Palace

As London grew and grew, it became clear that a bigger palace for the Royal Family was needed. So, in 1820, King George IV commissioned architect John Nash to transform Buckingham House into a magnificent palace.

However, the façade most people recognize, including the balcony where the Royal Family stand and wave, is much newer. It was designed by Sir Aston Webb and was completed in 1913. Webb used Portland Stone, a hardwearing limestone from Dorset. This replaced the older stonework, which was discoloured by pollution and was beginning to crumble.

St James's Palace is still the sovereign's official residence, but many monarchs have lived in Buckingham Palace. Queen Victoria was the first sovereign to live here and a giant memorial to her stands outside the Palace gates.

Sir Aston Webb

Queen Victoria (1837-1901)

King Edward VII (1901-10)

King George V (1910-36)

baked-clay. Many of these are decorated with sculptures of plants and animals. At the time, it was hoped that these would withstand the horrible sooty atmosphere of polluted Victorian London.

The twin towers either side of the main entrance are square at ground level but become octagonal further up. Behind these, Waterhouse created a cathedral-like main hall. With its monumental staircase and vast roof of steel and glass, this was used to display a number of complete dinosaur skeletons. These were wildly popular with Victorian visitors and still are today.

Sir Richard Owen

One of the most important people in the early days of the museum was the biologist and fossil-hunter Sir Richard Owen. He invented the word dinosaur, meaning 'terrible lizard'.

Charles Darwin

The newest extension is the cocoon-shaped Darwin Centre. It contains millions of specimens including Archie, a giant squid nearly nine metres long.

Buckingham House

It's hard to imagine now, but the most famous palace in the world was once a country house on the edge of London. The original house belonged to John Sheffield, who later became the Duke of Buckingham, which is how the palace gets its name. He lived there almost 300 years ago, and the site looked very different and was much smaller in size than it is today.

SIC SITI LÆ

Queen Charlotte

King George III

A flag called the Royal Standard flies when Her Majesty is at home. At other times the Union Jack is used.

Much of the decoration inside is in a lavish cream and gold style called Belle Époque.

Today, the enlarged palace has an incredible five miles of corridors, more than 1,500 doors and London's largest garden. As well as having 240 bedrooms and nearly 80 bathrooms, Her Majesty also has so many clocks that two people are employed just to wind them up!

Webb also designed the Mall, a grand ceremonial road running up to the palace like a grand red carpet. This is normally open to the public but is closed for processions on the great state occasions.

King Edward V111 (1936)

King George VI (1936-52)

Queen Elizabeth II (1952-)

In 1761 King George III bought Buckingham House for his wife, Queen Charlotte, as somewhere for their 15 children to live away from the noisy, crowded 18th-century city. It became known as 'The Queen's House'.

As the population increased, the capital expanded and new buildings began to surround the peaceful palace. However, the Royal Family kept residence there and, like London, Buckingham Palace started to grow.

Royal Courts of Justice

Another giant Victorian building, the Royal Courts of Justice required the destruction of dozens of streets, courtyards and alleyways and the demolition of more than 450 shops and slums. In all, more than six acres of central London were swept off the map and 4,125 people made homeless before it was built.

Over 11 years a massive new structure appeared on the site. As well as 24 new courtyards, the new building contained at least a thousand rooms and more than three miles of hallways and corridors. Building it consumed an estimated 35 million bricks in addition to the gleaming white stone of its famous façade.

The architect was George Edmund Street, whose Victorian Gothic style was hugely popular in the 19th century. Inside there are 60 individual courtrooms, and the oldest are arranged around a central hall.

George Edmund Street

As well as judges and lawyers the stonework incorporates carvings of wise men, such as Moses and Solomon from the Bible and the Anglo-Saxon king, Alfred the Great.

The building is so large that for a while someone actually moved into the basement without anyone realising he was living there.

The Royal Courts of Justice

Queen Victoria

This central hall is so large that when it is used for banquets there is room to seat more than 600 people for dinner.

Soaring stone arches, marble mosaic floors and beautiful stained glass windows, decorated with colourful coats of arms, helped to make the Royal Courts of Justice one of the most expensive buildings in London's 2,000-year history.

The coats of arms in the stained glass windows are those of past Lord Chancellors and Keepers of the Great Seal.

The Royal Courts of Justice

Chelsea Royal Hospital

Home to London's Chelsea Pensioners, the elegant, redbrick Royal Hospital was founded by Charles II for men who had retired from the British Army. The architect was Sir Christopher Wren, and it was the largest non-religious building he designed in his career.

Although construction work continued until 1692, the first retired soldiers arrived three years before that. Each was given a tiny wooden cabin in one of the long dormitory wings either side of a main block. Within this central block, Wren built a panelled dining hall and a beautiful chapel with views looking out across a beautiful lawn running down to the river. In the main courtyard is a statue of Charles II.

The building is really a retirement home rather than a hospital. Though retired, the residents come under the command of a military governor and are required

Once a year, on Founder's Day, the Pensioners hold a parade to celebrate Charles II's birthday. They are then inspected by a member of the Royal Family.

to be in uniform. The occupants wear a distinctive three-quarter length scarlet frock coat and an old fashioned tricorne hat.

Since Wren's day several other distinguished architects have worked to extend and improve the buildings. The early 19th century stable block was designed by Sir John Soane, designer of the old Bank of England, and more recently a medical centre was built for the soldiers by Quinlan Terry.

Chelsea Pensioners must be over the age of 65 and have served in the British Army. They must also be of 'good character' and not have any family who could look after them.

The Royal Hospital was originally only for men, but in 2009, after more than 300 years, the first two female Chelsea Pensioners were admitted.

The Royal Mews

In the 1800s the original King's Mews were demolished to make way for the National Gallery on Trafalgar Square. George IV had already begun to move his horses and ceremonial coaches to a site behind his new Buckingham Palace.

There was already an old riding school on site, called the Riding House. This had been designed in 1760 by Sir William Chambers but it was too small to accomodate all the King's horses. John Nash, who was already rebuilding the Palace, was asked to enlarge and improve the Royal Mews.

Beginning in 1824 Nash built a series of grand stables around the old riding school. Beneath a clock tower, a classical-style arch led into the main courtyard.

The Queen has more than 70 different carriages. These include the Gold State Coach, which was built for George III in 1762. It weighs more than four tons and needs eight horses to pull it!

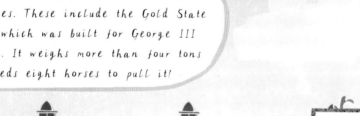

Sir William Chambers

The newest coach on display is the Golden Jubilee State Coach, which was built in 2012. It is only the second carriage to be built for the Royal Family in more than 100 years.

40

Coach houses on one side provided accommodation for stable staff and on the opposite side Nash created stables for around 50 horses, along with rooms for food and for saddles and harnesses. The Royal Mews is also used to store the uniforms worn by the royal coachmen.

The Royal Mews was extended again for Queen Victoria, who owned nearly 200 horses. New buildings included a forge for the royal farrier (whose job it was to shoe the animals) and a school for his children and those of the other servants to attend.

The buildings may be old but they are used for a more modern purpose. In addition to Her Majesty's 30 horses, this is where the royal car collection is kept and maintained.

John Nash

Queen Victoria

King George IV

Queen Elizabeth II learned to ride at the Royal Mews when she was four years old. She had lessons on a Shetland pony called Peggy, which had been given to her by her grandfather, George V. She called him 'Grandpa England'.

41

The Royal Observatory

Scientists in the 17th century were very interested in the stars and in 1675 Charles II appointed John Flamsteed as the first ever Astronomer Royal.

A new Royal Observatory was planned, overlooking the Thames at Greenwich. The King agreed to pay for this, giving £500 to the project and permission for bricks to be salvaged from an old fortress at Tilbury in Essex.

Sir Christopher Wren designed a building 'for the observer's habitation'. The main room was octagonal in shape, with a high ceiling to permit the use of telescopes and clocks with longer pendulums for extra accuracy. Surprisingly, the Astronomer Royal had to pay for his own equipment. He used this equipment to make more than 30,000 observations, which helped him draw maps of the stars, which were published after his death.

In 1833 a device called a time ball was installed on top of a small turret and was dropped at precisely one o'clock each afternoon. It is still there today, enabling ships' captains on the river to set their clocks accurately before setting off on a voyage.

In Wren's day Greenwich was in the countryside but the expansion of Victorian London and increased air pollution meant that by the 1940s the scientists had to move elsewhere.

Wren was the perfect architect for the project. He worked on a number of famous buildings such as St Paul's Cathedral, but he was also Professor of Astronomy at the University of Oxford.

Sir Christopher Wren

42

Time Ball

The research done here
was hugely important because
knowledge of the stars and
accurate timekeeping were
essential for early explorers
and navigators.

The brass strip set into the ground outside the Observatory
marks the Prime or Greenwich Meridian. International time
zones around the world have been measured from this point
since 1884. Standing astride this line you have one foot in the
Earth's eastern hemisphere and one in the western hemisphere.

John Flamsteed

43

Somerset House

Built around a large and spectacular central courtyard, Somerset House takes its name from the Dukes of Somerset. The Somersets were one of several powerful aristocratic families whose luxurious riverside palaces occupied this stretch of the Thames during the medieval and Tudor periods.

In 1552 the first Duke of Somerset was accused of treason and was then beheaded. His palace was taken by the King, Edward VI, and was used by the Royal Family for the next 200 years. By 1775 it was no longer needed and was knocked down. The government asked architect Sir William Chambers to build London's first ever office block in its place.

The new Somerset House was enormous, with great Neoclassical wings, designed to look like a series of Georgian townhouses. A statue of George III stood

Today the courtyard is one of London's most popular open spaces. It is used for showing films and staging concerts. Each December the fountains are switched off and covered by a large ice-skating arena.

in the central courtyard and the building's decorative stonework was supplied by several of the leading artists of the time.

With so much space to fill, several arts and science organisations moved in, including the Royal Academy and the Royal Society. The Navy took one-and-a-half wings of the building to give them direct access to the river. Government departments occupied much of the rest and remained here until the beginning of this century.

Today the building has been reborn as an important centre for the arts. It incorporates several galleries, the Courtauld Institute of Art and a museum.

Until the Victoria Embankment was built in the 1860s it was possible to arrive at Somerset House by boat. A golden state barge belonging to a senior naval commissioner is on display in the basement.

45

St Pancras Station

One of the greatest monuments from the Victorian railway age, this engineering marvel of brick, glass and iron is still in use. Today high-speed Eurostar trains travel from here through the Channel Tunnel to Paris.

The train shed covering the platforms was designed by William Barlow and measures nearly 213 metres end to end. To clear the platforms the shed had to be 73 metres wide but with trains running below there was no room for pillars or columns.

TO THE TRAINS

The railway platforms had to be raised six metres above ground level because of the nearby Regent's Canal. Barlow arranged for the space below the platform to be used to store barrels of beer arriving by train from the Midlands.

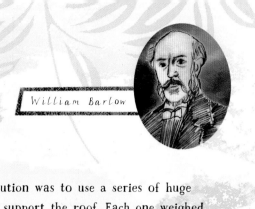

William Barlow

Sir George Gilbert Scott

Barlow's solution was to use a series of huge metal 'ribs' to support the roof. Each one weighed an incredible 55 tons and when it was completed in 1867 the shed was the largest single-span building anywhere in the world.

The front of the station included a luxury hotel called the Midland Grand and was designed by

Sir George Gilbert Scott in a fashionable style derived from Italian Gothic. He had planned to build something similar for the government but thought his design was a bit too grand for a railway hotel. The hotel was certainly impressive. There was gold leaf on the walls, hydraulic lifts, and fireplaces in all the rooms.

In the 1960s both hotel and station were due to be demolished. Fortunately, campaigners led by the poet John Betjeman managed to save what are now recognized as two of the greatest Victorian buildings in London.

Scott's son and grandson were also successful architects. His grandson, Giles Gilbert Scott, is probably most famous for designing the classic red telephone box.

St Paul's Cathedral

It is astonishing to think that, for all its immense size and magnificence, the building that St Paul's Cathedral replaced was actually both taller and longer.

What we now call Old St Paul's was destroyed during the Great Fire of London in 1666. It had been built by the Normans nearly 600 years earlier, on Ludgate Hill, which was the highest point in what was then a walled city.

It might have been possible to repair the damaged cathedral, but it was decided that a new one would be built instead. Sir Christopher Wren was asked to undertake the task, even though he was already working hard to replace more than 50 of the 89 smaller churches, which had also been destroyed in the fire.

Before work began, Wren produced a scale model showing what he was planning. This still exists and is six metres long. It is made of oak and is tall enough for a person to walk through.

Building the brand new cathedral took 35 years. The huge cost of the build was paid for by the government, using a new tax on coal.

Wren chose a style called Baroque and designed a dome in place of the old tower and spire. In fact, he cleverly designed a double-dome — one was intended to be seen from inside the building, and above this a taller one which could only be seen from outside. From the top it is possible to see one of his other ingenious tricks: a series of false outer walls which conceal the huge stone buttresses that are needed to support the building.

Sir Christopher Wren

As the building neared completion Wren was so old he had to be hoisted to the top in a basket. When he died in 1723, aged 89, he was one of the first people to be buried in the crypt.

At one point during construction the work stopped because an earthquake in Dorset interrupted the supply of white Portland stone.

49

Tate Britain

When it was decided to move out of most of the British art from the National Gallery in Trafalgar Square, a new home was built for it overlooking the river in Pimlico.

The building was paid for by Sir Henry Tate, who made his fortune refining and selling sugar. Tate also agreed to donate 67 paintings and three valuable sculptures to the new gallery.

The first architect to work on the new gallery was Sidney Smith. The site had originally been occupied by a gigantic prison called the Millbank Penitentiary. Once the eight-sided prison building was closed in 1890, Smith began work on the project.

Sidney Smith

Meet 500 Years of British Art

Sir Henry Tate

Rex Whistler

Tate Britain was the first public gallery in the country to have its own restaurant. This is decorated with colourful murals painted by Rex Whistler.

Before long other wealthy men were following Tate's example, donating money and works of art to the gallery. This meant the building had to be enlarged several times, and over the next 100 years other architects were brought in to make alterations and extensions.

The most recent extension is James Stirling's colourful postmodern wing, which contrasts strongly with the old Victorian and Edwardian structures. Named the Clore Gallery, it contains paintings by one of Britain's most important artists, J.M.W. Turner.

Many of the floors inside are specially reinforced to withstand the weight of heavy bronze and marble sculptures.

James Stirling

Meet 500 Years of British Art

When the Tate's paintings were removed during the Second World War, one was found to be too large to move. Instead, a brick wall was built around it to protect it from enemy bombers.

J.M.W. Turner

David Hockney

Tower Bridge

Instantly recognized around the world, in 1894 Tower Bridge became the first bridge to be built downriver from London Bridge.

Its novel lifting mechanism was devised by Horace Jones so that large vessels could pass through. The engineering needed to achieve this was highly advanced for the time and contrasted strongly with the ornate Gothic architectural style of the bridge. It was hoped that this style would help the bridge to blend in with the nearby Tower of London. Building it took eight years, 11,000 tons of steel and 31,000,000 bricks. The metalwork was held together by two million rivets and covered in

In 1968, a young RAF pilot was arrested after flying low over Parliament in his Hawker Hunter jet and then between the towers of Tower Bridge.

22,000 litres of brown paint. (The modern red, white and blue colour scheme was introduced in 1977 to celebrate Queen Elizabeth II's Silver Jubilee.)

The bridge was originally operated by steam power, but about 40 years ago it began using electricity. Each of the lifting sections, known as bascules, weighs around 1,000 tons. Raising them takes only five minutes, which is lucky as this happens about 20 times a week!

High above the river, twin walkways were designed so pedestrians could cross over the river while the bridge was raised. Today, visitors can look down on the traffic while standing on a section of reinforced-glass floor.

The bascules are lifted only as high as they need to be for the boat to pass through safely. The only exception is when the Queen is on the river. When this happens both sections are raised as high as possible to salute Her Majesty.

In 1952 the driver of a No. 78 bus full of passengers had to jump the gap when the bridge began to open as he was driving across. He was awarded £10 for his bravery.

Ships always have priority over cars and on at least one occasion the President of the United States has been kept waiting for the bridge to reopen!

53

Tower of London

For nearly a thousand years this mighty fortress has towered over London. The Tower was built as part of William the Conqueror's display of strength and superiority after he invaded England in 1066.

The oldest part of the castle is the central keep or White Tower. It was probably built around 20 years after the invasion and was given its name because the limestone walls were once painted white to make it look even larger and more impressive. The basic layout is still as it was in the 13th century but there are now no fewer than 22 different towers!

The Tower has been used for a number of different functions, not all of them military. It is still a royal palace. But different parts have been used as a prison, an astronomical observatory, a mint for manufacturing money, a strong room for the Crown Jewels, and even a zoo!

At night the Tower is locked during the Ceremony of the Keys. This is the oldest military ceremony in the world and has taken place every night since the 14th century. The occasion has been delayed only once, in 1940, when it was interrupted by an air raid.

The smallest cell in the White Tower dungeons is called the Little Ease. It is so small that prisoners could not stand, sit comfortably or lie down.

Thought to be worth around £20 billion, the Crown Jewels were once stolen by an Irishman called Colonel Blood. They were quickly recovered and amazingly Charles II then pardoned Blood – although no one really knows why!

ENTRY TO THE TRAITORS' GATE

Guy Fawkes

The Royal Menagerie or zoo was based here until Victorian times. Animals on show included lions, an elephant and a polar bear, which had a long chain so it could fish in the Thames. Most were presents from foreign rulers.

Prisoners held in the Tower during its long history include Queen Elizabeth I, Adolf Hitler's deputy Rudolf Hess, and Guy Fawkes.

Victoria & Albert Museum

The original buildings for the Victoria and Albert Museum were constructed out of corrugated iron and glass and were so ugly that they were nicknamed the 'Brompton Boilers'.

In 1890 it was decided to rebuild the museum and a competition was held amongst leading architects to find the best design. The winner was Sir Aston Webb. The majestic façade and lofty tower of his design were thought to characterise the immense scale, wealth and magnificence of the British Empire.

Victoria was queen when the project began but completing it took so long that by the time the museum reopened in 1909 her son Edward VII was on the throne.

The museum was built using a combination of red brick, decorative mosaic portraits of famous artists, and a type of fired clay called terracotta. Behind the museum's great bronze doors vast collections of furniture, tapestries and other objects from around the world were displayed.

The statue on the top of the museum is of a character called 'Fame', but for some reason her nose is missing.

When the museum flooded in the 1980s, hundreds of damaged books were put in the freezers at Harrods while they were waiting to be restored.

Queen Victoria & Prince Albert

The museum today is so large that the walk around the outside is more than a third of a mile long. Exhibits include the world's oldest carpet (from 1549) and a full-sized replica of Trajan's Column, an ancient Roman monument that is so tall it is displayed in two halves. Visitors can also see the first ever Christmas card, which was invented by the museum's founding director, Sir Henry Cole.

Sir Aston Webb

During the First World War the museum's guidebook was printed in French to make it more welcoming to refugees from France and Belgium.

Sir Henry Cole

In the early days the museum did not employ any guides. Instead soldiers and police officers showed visitors around the various galleries.

Westminster Abbey

This is a site brimming full of history – Roman remains have been found here, and William the Conqueror was crowned here on Christmas Day in 1066. The present abbey was built in the mid-13th century and was dedicated to St Peter. The first builder was probably Henry of Rheims although it has been extended since his day.

Everything about the abbey is breathtakingly grand, from the 31-metre-tall nave to the soaring towers added by Nicholas Hawksmoor in the 18th century. It has been the setting for almost every coronation, royal wedding and funeral.

Inside Henry VII's Lady Chapel is an outstanding example of the Perpendicular style. Its elaborate fan-vaulted ceiling and huge areas of glass are two of the greatest achievements of 16th century craftsmanship.

The abbey contains more than 3,000 memorials to kings, queens, and nationally important men and women. However, by far the most remarkable is the Tomb of the Unknown Warrior, the grave of an ordinary soldier killed in the Great War. As no one knows his identity, he has come to represent every father, son and brother who never came home from the First World War.

William the Conqueror

ALFRED, LORD TENNYSON

CHARLES DICKENS

RUDYARD KIPLING

BEN JONSON

LAURENCE OLIVIER

SIR ISAAC NEWTON

GEOFFREY CHAUCER

The 13th century floor in front of the altar is known as the Cosmati Pavement. It is made of thousands of mosaic pieces from Italy and, according to one medieval interpretation, the pattern can be used to calculate when the universe will come to an end.

Some of the money to build St Paul's Cathedral came from Westminster Abbey. This is believed to be the origin of the saying, 'robbing Peter to pay Paul'.

Famous writers and artists have traditionally been buried in an area known as Poets' Corner. Ben Jonson, who died in 1673, was given such a small plot that he had to be buried standing up.

The strangest statue in the abbey is probably the one of St Wilgefortis. According to legend, she grew a beard to avoid getting married.

QUEEN ELIZABETH I

HENRY PURCELL

MARY, QUEEN OF SCOTS

CHARLES DARWIN

THOMAS HARDY

THE UNKNOWN WARRIOR

London Today

London is continually evolving. To meet the demands of a growing population, the skyline is changing all the time, as old buildings are demolished and replaced with exciting new ones.

Advanced technology and clever engineering means towers can be built taller than ever, and many have been given nicknames based on the unusual shapes created by their architects. The likes of the Gherkin, Cheesegrater and Walkie-Talkie have become quite famous, often before they were completed.

A trip to the top of one of London's skyscrapers is always an adventure. On a clear day you can see for miles, right across London and even as far as the countryside beyond.

55 Broadway, London's first ever highrise building, is only 15 storeys tall. When it was finished in 1929 the Fire Brigade banned anyone from using the upper floors because none of their ladders could reach that high!

Kings Cross

BT Tower

Nelson's Column

Soho

Northbank

Westminster

Southb...

55 Broadway

Oxo Tower

Royal Albert Hall

Chelsea

Vauxhall

London Eye

Lambeth

Battersea Power Station

Clapham

Clerkenwell

Cheesegrater

The Gherkin looks a bit like a giant pickle or a rocket and is one of the few circular buildings in London.

Tower Hamlets

Stratford

Velodrome

Gherkin

arbican

The strange shape of the Walkie-Talkie means the upper floors are larger than the lower ones. At the top is the Sky Garden, an indoor garden with spectacular views across the river.

The velodrome in east London, the indoor cycle track used for the London Olympics, has been nicknamed the Pringle because of its swooping, curved shape.

Walkie-Talkie

City

Canary Wharf

O2 Arena

Shakespeare's Globe

Isle of Dogs

The O2 Arena in Greenwich was originally known as the Millennium Dome. It is so large that New York's Statue of Liberty could easily fit inside.

Tate Modern

outhvark

The Mayor of London's City Hall looks a bit like a crash helmet. It doesn't have a front or back and the shape is designed to be energy efficient. Compared to a squarer building it stays cooler in summer and warmer in winter.

Cutty Sark

Greenwich

The Shard is easily London's tallest building at 309 metres. On a clear, sunny day it is possible to see for about 40 miles from the 72nd floor.

VIVM·LARGITAS·PERFECIT.

Peckham

London Transport

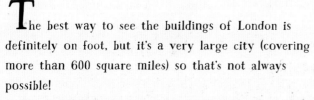

The best way to see the buildings of London is definitely on foot, but it's a very large city (covering more than 600 square miles) so that's not always possible!

In the 19th century London became the first place in the world to have an underground railway, and 150 years later more than 1.3 billion journeys a year are still made by Tube. The Tube has nearly 260 miles of track, 270 stations, and well over 400 escalators. There are also around 40 disused or 'ghost' stations – you can sometimes spot these through the windows of a moving train.

London is famous for its black cabs. Drivers have to take a test called the Knowledge. To pass this they need to memorise an incredible 25,000 street names and over 320 different routes around the city.

The view of the city is much better from the top deck of one of London's famous red double-deckers. Horses pulled the first double-decker buses. Nowadays, most buses are steered by a driver, but there have been trials of small driverless electric buses in a few places.

An increasingly popular way to move around the crowded streets and a brilliant way to view London's beautiful buildings is by bicycle. You can rent one very cheaply or ride your own on the growing number of cycle lanes, which criss-cross around the capital.

Another option is to take a river bus along the Thames, and many Londoners now travel to work every day by water. You can whizz past the Houses of Parliament, spot the dome of St. Paul's Cathedral and duck under Tower Bridge.

London Underground
Oyster card Bicycle Docklands Light Railway
Cable Car Bus Mind the gap!
DLR Black Cab Walk Travelcard
River Bus TFL Cycle Hire
Tube Thames Clipper
Tram Taxi National Rail

Bloomsbury Children's Books
An imprint of Bloomsbury Publishing Plc

50 Bedford Square
London
WC1B 3DP
UK

1385 Broadway
New York
NY 10018
USA

www.bloomsbury.com

BLOOMSBURY and the Diana logo are trademarks of Bloomsbury Publishing Plc

First published in Great Britain 2018

A catalogue record for this book is available from the British Library.

Library of Congress Cataloguing-in-Publication data has been applied for.

ISBN
HB: 9781408883648

2 4 6 8 10 9 7 5 3

Printed and bound in China by Leo Paper Products, Heshan, Guangdong

MIX
Paper from
responsible sources
FSC
www.fsc.org   FSC® C020056

To find out more about our authors and books visit www.bloomsbury.com.
Here you will find extracts, author interviews, details of forthcoming
events and the option to sign up for our newsletters.

The National Archives is the official archives and publisher for the UK Government,
and for England and Wales. We work to bring together and secure the future of the
public record, both digital and physical, for future generations.

The National Archives is open to all, offering a range of activities and spaces
to enjoy, as well as our readingrooms for research. Many of our
most popular records are also available online.

nationalarchives.gov.uk
Twitter: @UKNatArchives
Facebook: The National Archives